This Book Belongs to:

CHANCERS
GARDEN

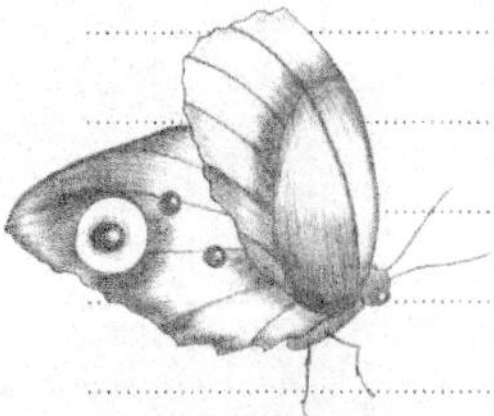

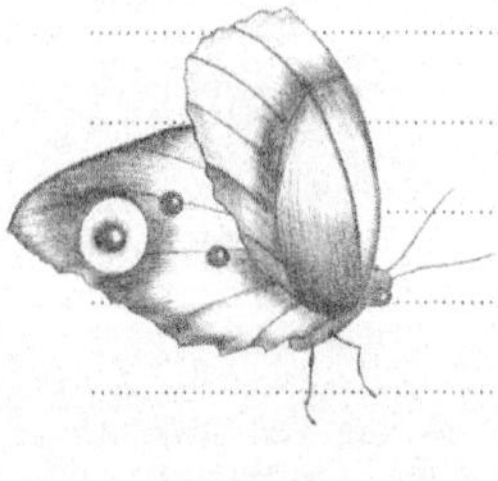

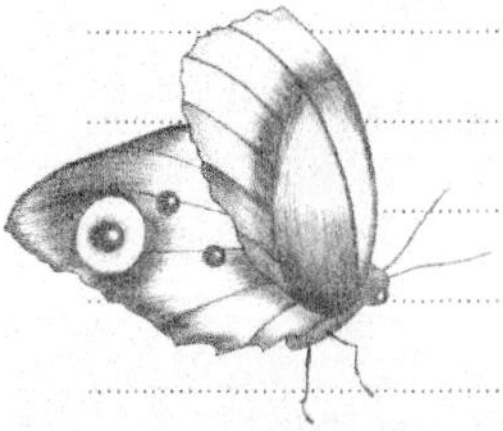

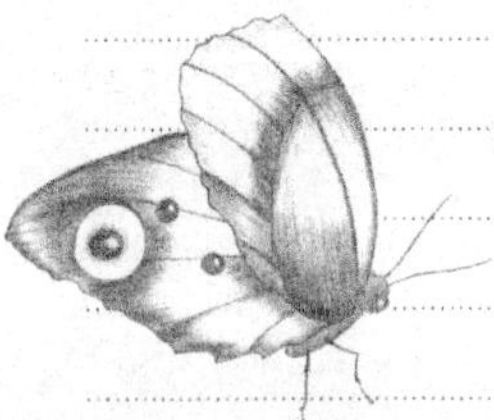

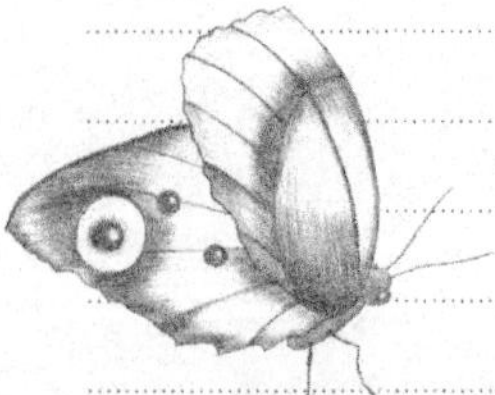

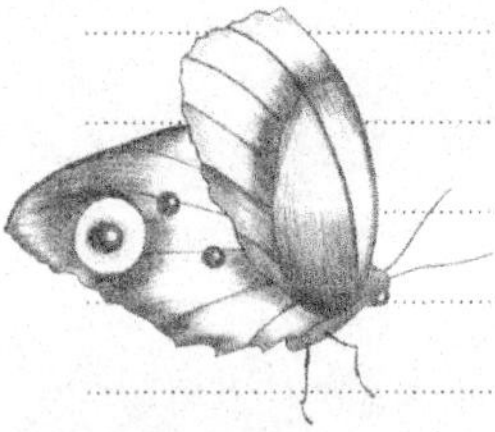

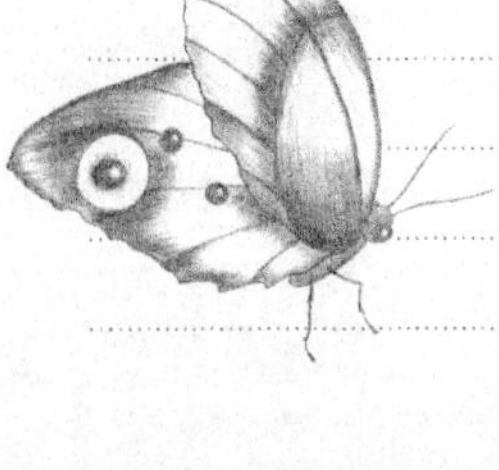

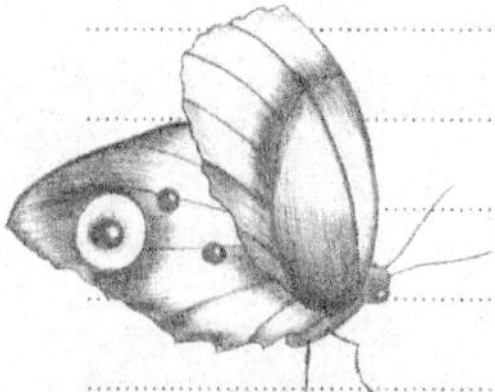

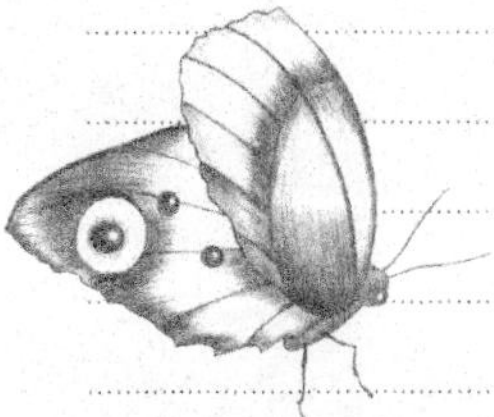

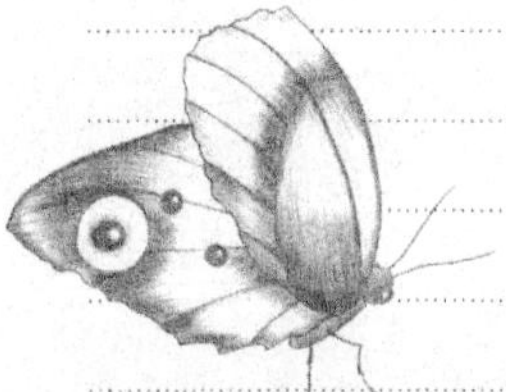

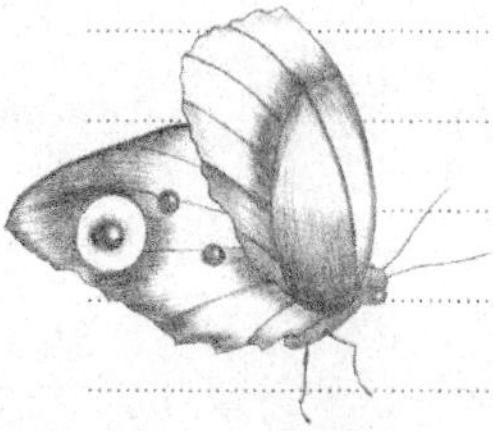

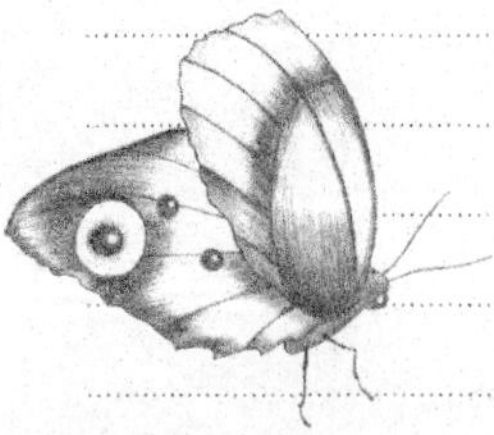

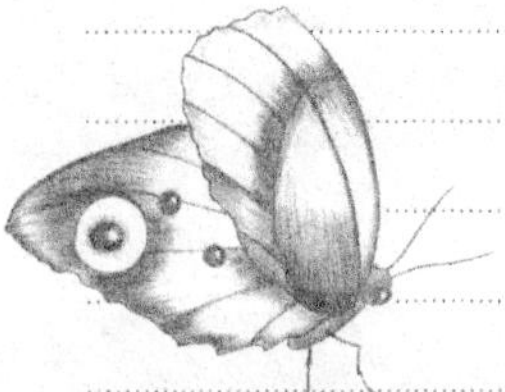

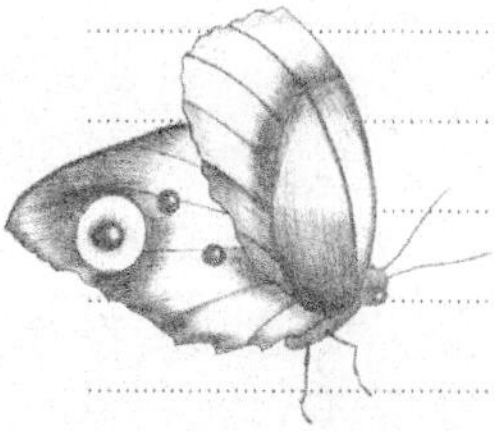

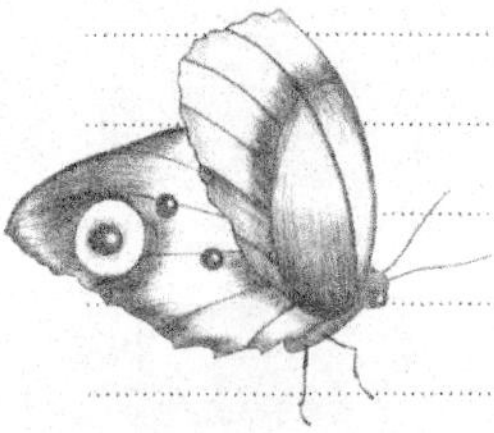

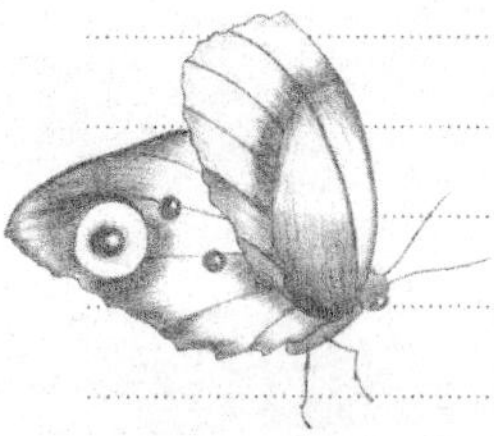

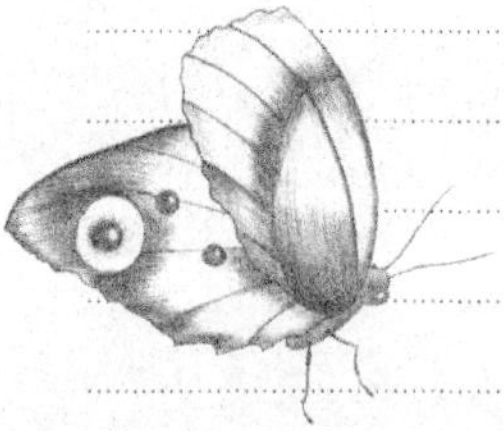

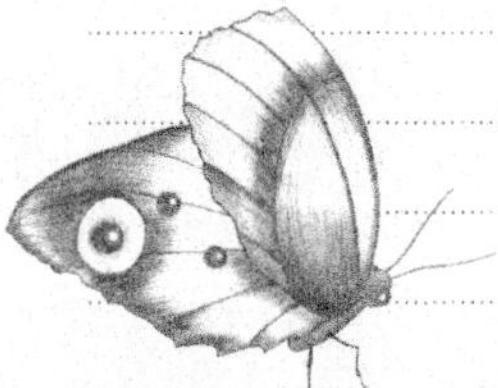

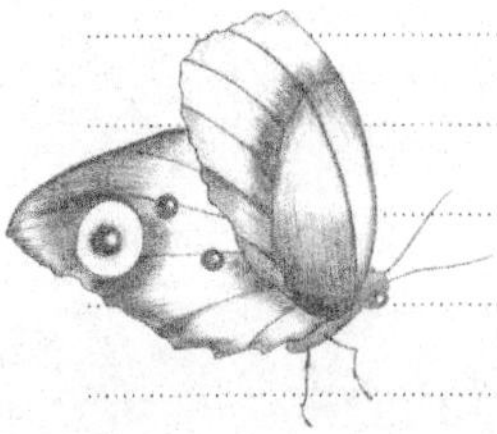

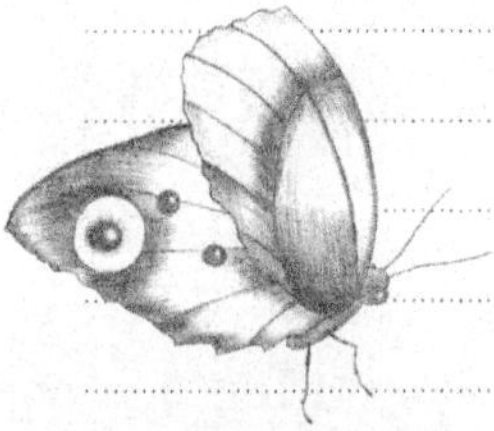

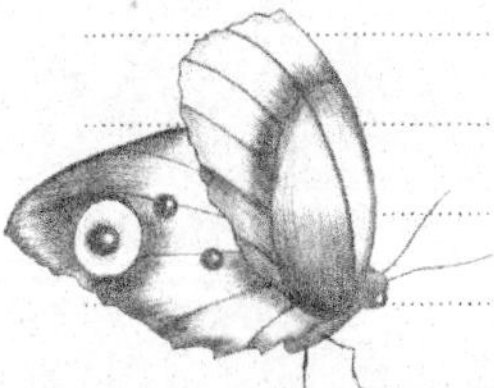

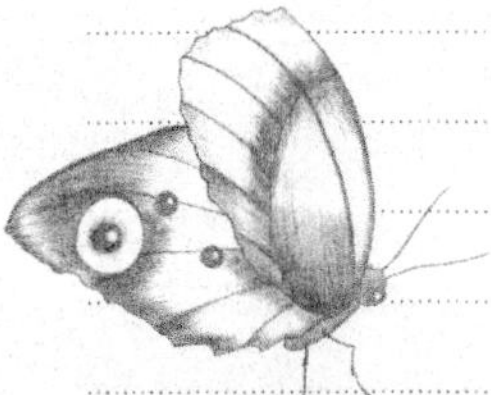

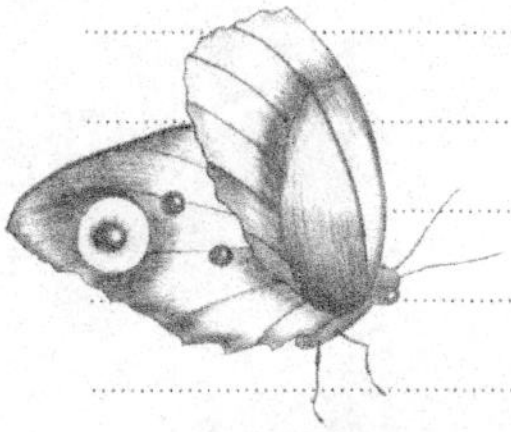

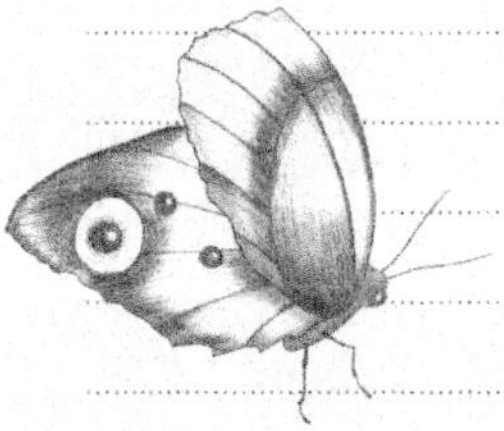

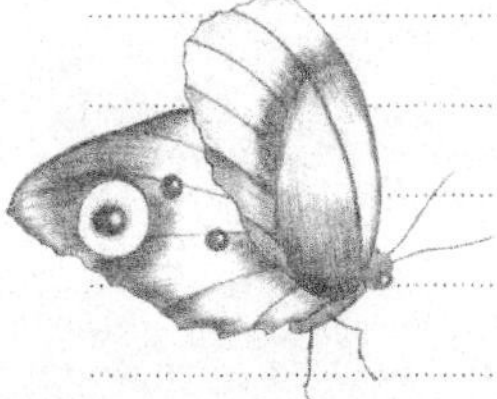

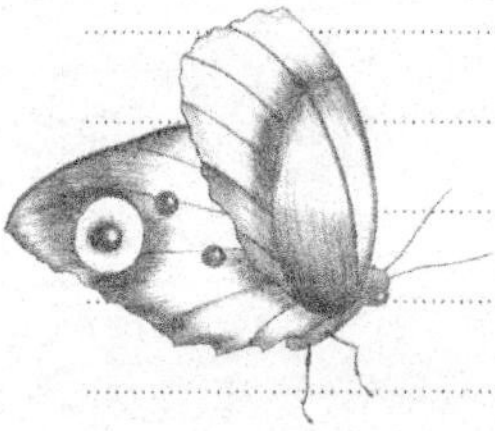

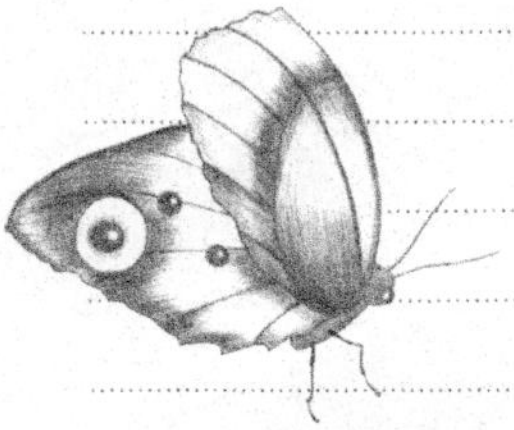

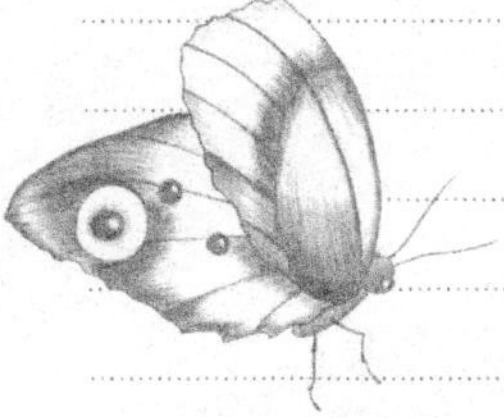

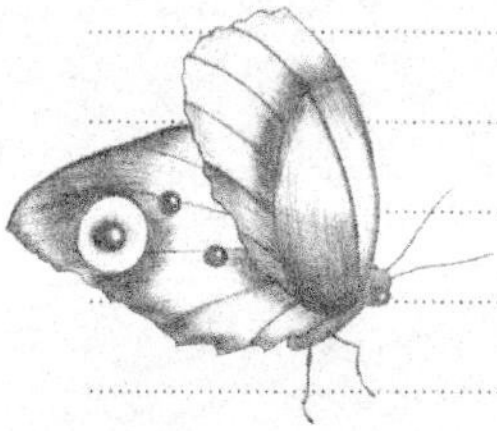

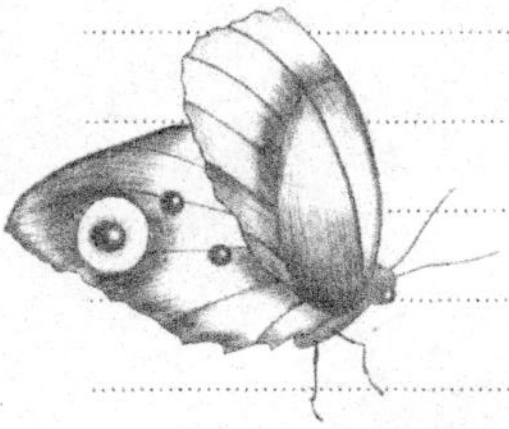

Printed in Great Britain
by Amazon

54126647R00069